DARKNESS UNDER THE TREES/WALKING
BEHIND THE SPANISH

DARKNESS UNDER THE TREES/WALKING BEHIND THE SPANISH

Luis Omar Salinas

Chicano Studies Library Publications
University of California, Berkeley
1982

ISBN: 0-918520-04-5

Some of these poems have appeared in *Poetry East, Columbia, Backwash, Plum,* and *Revista Chicano-Riqueña.*

This collection was edited by Christopher Buckley. Additional revisions were made by Jon Veinberg and Gary Soto.

The book was designed by Carolyn Soto and produced under the direction of Francisco García-Ayvens.

We are grateful for the technical support and use of facilities extended by Berkeley's Humanities Computing Service, under the direction of Ann Hernandez.

Inkworks

DARKNESS UNDER THE TREES

WALKING BEHIND THE SPANISH

DARKNESS UNDER THE TREES

I

On My Birth

From my birth on
I've been on an adventure,
happy go lucky
at the bingo parties
and at pot lucks.
My three year old sister
cracked a tequila bottle
over my head;
I was a year older,
wiser but not as valiant.
My mother's death
caused a great scar--
one that has not healed
to this day.
I guess dying is another
way of saying goodbye,
another way of living;
not being able to say
hello the next morning.
I guess we're all crazy
in our own way.
It would take a violinist
to figure out my madness,
and an accordionist
to make me fit for a wedding.
What I want to do is
tell you about my wounds
and place a few yellow flowers
on your kitchen table;
then I will smoke a cigarette

and go with my imagination
to the stars, singing
Catholic hymns, a bit dazed,
a little wiser than last time
still unsure but gently dedicated.

This Dreaming Morning

Morning comes like a bashful
barmaid, pregnant and witty.
I drink sunlight
with the early swallows
and conjure the eyes of
a madonna.
A woman pauses on the avenue--
with an interesting
face one can go anywhere.
Yellow time
passes
like a horse's rump.
These feet keep tune
to the nonsense,
I go gouge the eyelashes
of trees,
a soft breeze
goes unemployed, invisible,
stretching its hand
through the insomnia
of light.
And I am a friend
to this dreaming morning.
I shall place a vase of flowers
upon its head.

I'm On My Way

Evening becomes evening,
and I'm not letting up, God.
I'm still sleeping
with my neighbor's wife
on Sundays--
and sometimes drive nails
into flowers out of boredom
and bump into beggars
when morning goes dead.
Oh, mischief like a thief
cutting roses, presenting
them to choir girls...
I'll make it
to heaven on a motorbike yet--
beardless Leo Da Vinci
singing Spanish folk songs.

I Go Dreaming Roads in My Youth

I'm not interested in the poverty
of ignorance and its songs,
to be generous to myself is my song;
I will give my shirt to no one
even though I talk too much and
give my words to the ungrateful
they will not find a home in my thoughts.

I put on my hat, stride forward,
act, dream, love; I take a drink
and let fame touch me, yet in the end
I'll place it to rest.

When I raise my arm to the populace
I raise it with sincerity
and pride in my monstrous vitality.
When the world clubs me
I shall fight back, if it loves me
I will love back, if it steps in my
shadow's fortune, I will give thanks
to God and those who surround me.

I have many stories, a haughty dramatist
weaving scenes of optimism, of alegria,
of romance. The world is too tired
and little concerned with pathos or
the consequences of tragedy.
What is important is the eloquence
of a river and a boy pushing a boat
into the water, a white dove gently
from the hands of his mother and
a clumsy serenade dreaming the afternoon.

Today, I like this world, and
if your life is worth nothing, don't sing,
don't come to my door with broken hearts
and complaints. Today, I go dreaming
roads in my youth.

Salinas Wakes Early and Goes to the Park to Lecture Sparrows

Little philosophers
of the twig,
gaunt adventurers of philanthropy,
you understand I'm from sturdy
merchant stock.

I've taken violin lessons
from the trash collector,
six lessons in six weeks,
and I sold it and turned to you
hard workers of the light.

I turn down the road
beating the dust
from my coattails,
dust that smells of you.

Beaks like musicians
looking for work,
I'm reminded of far off
music from a girl's lips
drawn to your sounds
under the October sky.

I woke early to remind
you of your chores
little pay and sadness,
of your duties to God
and lovers.

Now I'm off to study chess
and bellies of cows dreaming milk.
And like the mariachi
I look at the sun,
drum a gourd
and go dreaming into the afternoon

happy to unfold this spirit
which aches from the ashes
of sweat and moonlight.
I adore your freedom
and when unhappy
watch your flight
into my dark conjecturing.

I Toss Smiles toward the Open Sea

What is happening to me?
I ask as love
builds its fingers
of snow over my heart.

It is like the raindrops
of silk over a woman
who smiles often
and is fortunate
at dusk.

And I pale over the window
of life, waiting by the elms
for the sparrows that
spring from my heart
into the night air.

Air of guitars
and deaf mutes,
air of laughter
knifed in the air
by swallows
who understand
my loneliness.

Into the night of darkness
and pirates, drummers off
to Europe, I create delight
and smile towards the open sea,
calm, like a stranger
grieving a little,
out to sea for the last
time.

Coming Back from It

I've been thinking about falling
in love, but the weather has been harsh,
a hair shirt of sorts, some ashes,
and I've noticed
a blind leaf fall on my black boots.
I catch my breath, lift
my white handkerchief up to my face
and look at my palm, where ambition crosses
and recrosses like the traffic at 5:00.

The cat from up the street
breaks toward a bird
and the sunlight catches
at my pulse
like a leaf puzzled in the air.

In Mazatlán
(After a vision of Shelley being cremated at the edge
    of the Mexican coast)

Being a bachelor is crazy business,
    in Mazatlan I thought I was the Mexican
    Shelley. And casting glances
        at the Primavera seagulls
    I lost myself there--
        like a deep afternoon sky.
I left my heart
    standing among the people
    in their revolution
        of joy
    and dog-beaten
        saludos.
My bones singing to Shelley
    in his awful voyage
    as the Mayan Gods
        spear in hands
watch from a distance,
    and I cavort
        among the maidens.
I take myself there
    a visionary
among tales of fortune
    and disillusionment.
And toss my soul
    like a madman
        trying to emulate
        scholarly diction,
and flounder
    in the waves,
ghost in the horizon.

13

I toss these festered arms
into political blunders
and poetic anarchy
professing a kinship
with the sea.
This bachelor of little eloquence
has a fate to surrender to
and in the quiet whispers
of morning,
walks with legendary
poetic heroes,
watching the sun rise
like a mother.
It takes a fool to be a poet;
an evil wonder lies at bay,
goodbye Mazatlan,
you have surrendered to me
like a woman,
throwing her blouse into the sea.

That My Name Is Omar

I suffer that my name is Omar Salinas.
That I want to touch someone in the
incredible loneliness of nights.
That I frighten away those I should
be close to. I suffer when I go crazy
and can't love anyone. Whether it
is Tuesday or Sunday, I suffer.
I suffer a lust for fame and
immortality. That I tried to
commit suicide. That I have
compassion for the unfortunate.
I suffer the death of matrimony.
The death of my mother.
The eyes of God.
I want to understand this and that
and come up with zero.
What should I do
but walk and look at the lovely sky?

Testament

My mother passed away,
my second mother
was good to me,
and I became a poet;
that should be enough
to close my eyes.
One afternoon I'll go
to the sea,
and at last,
on a Sunday or Thursday,
I'll have found my home.
I just want them
to bury me near
my benevolent mother.
This I've left written,
and I suffer for not
being more generous.

II

Autumn

for Peter everwine

Autumn again fluttering
silvery wings,
the finches gather
in the garden
like troubled peasants.
And I'm the peasant
without dreams
looking on--
Here all secrets
jump out of my head,
desperation plays
a distant violin.
Oh, that I were
a ghost dancing
a world of bells,
listening to the agony,
and a fistful
of tenderness
from my absent mother.

Early Death

in memoriam Ben Durazo

The rain tonight
reminds me of you,
silent friend,
taken in the alabaster
tolling afternoon.
The sun was leaving--
only the sun comes back.

I feel like beating up philosophers,
or putting on a ghost's long shirt
to search you out in this tempest--
no use. No one wants anything
to do with the dead.

There,
in the afterlife,
your face will shine
like an orange moon.

Late Evening Conversation with My Friend's Dog, Moses, after Watching Visconti's *The Innocent*

Moses, who is there to save us
from the crickets, those small gods
in armor, nagging some vague truths
transient as Visconti's light
through the arbors of grape and lilac?
I think the loquats have been sleeping
like our guardian angels and
who is to say what the moon is thinking?
Or the lost fragments of our hearts?
It could all be the end of air
in liquor, rain, or self indulgence.
You could complain about each leaf
of the apricot, falling. I too
could catalog each woman that failed
to save me, and we both could be
as melancholy as clouds. Moses,
there are no prophecies in the sky,
only this earth, its grey at our
fingertips. Let's stop bitching
about death and the light of the lovers
on the veranda next door. I want
to explain, as you should too, about
the meekness of all the nights that
have passed, burnt-out stars or storms.
We must take control of the air
and breathe as only we can
like the icy throat of comets.
Listen to me Moses, we're not
as Biblical as rain, but our transgressions
go to the sea in search of speech.
Salt or otherwise, blood or otherwise,
things remain the same so long as we watch
the fiddles turn. And despite the women,
the rise and fall of French cinema,
the heart must dance like lightning,
burn, and save itself.

Salinas Summering at the Caspian and Thinking of Hamlet

I get up and consider my corduroy coat
the collar tattered as Christianity;
they bring me several figs, a tangerine,
and rolls printed with a cross--
Is this what troubles are about?
I genuflect toward the sea,
whisper songs I learned in French
and throw crumbs to the seagulls
and anything hovering in the air.

There are boats with the red sails
of the past, and grey hulls approaching.
My pockets are thin and bulged as
a flatterer. As I put the coat on
I'm full of high sentence, or
I'm someone behind a curtain
overhearing the indiscretions
of the rich and courtly, or
the equal debate of flies.
I would have a play of sonorous maidens
asleep, orchids and gardenias
floating moon-like on the pond,
hearts left to the idiocyncrisies of youth...

Here the rivers are frozen,
the graves are dug in early spring;
my mind drifts to a courtyard
of children and their games against
the state. The next time I put on
my coat or hat and plan the downfall
or outcome of anything I'll have to
duel with the sunlight,

as pure as any of us
after the poisons and bad teeth
of love. What I want is a
white orange and the perpetual eye
of the glacier which sees one way
slowly and is blind to our tin
souls. Nevertheless, it's the snow
and my old shoes I glimpse at
like old women.
               I step into it all
as if I were relieved of considerations
and the cacophony of mothers
admonishing us for our melancholy
hold on the wine glass--
this is something I know well among
the ice and small deposits of romance.
I know the blank music of the clouds
as well as I know my hands against
the window of my paramour--she is a
songless thrush and her cry is
the blue ink of night, the blood
returning to my heart with its air
beside the Caspian Sea, or any blue
far from here. I would meet her
and offer the inconsequence of
meager gloves at her breast,
the salt on our lips.

What else I ask myself do the rags
of flesh and minds ask for?
There is speech, and it comes now
in the form of swords or flames,
or it doesn't come at all.

Fragments for Fall
for Delmore Schwartz

September--
here I am, growing old
with the trees, bitter
about the lovely
ways of women
and the air hewn
with a light smoke
as they pass.

*

Lying in the park
with a squirrel
that's not afraid
of my hand,
imagining
a woman who's not afraid
of my life...
my feelings condense
like a cloud
about to go
into the blue.

*

I leave the house
with an umbrella
and one shoe,
and sing
in the grove

to the bankers
in their bowler hats.
I celebrate myself
in several newspapers
like a bear
at a honey log.
All morning
I'm Hamlet
mooning over history
and the voices
behind a row of elms
are mad as flies.

*

My feelings skip
like the wind
in a deaf tune
I roll in the grass,
some hero of the past
has a hand on
my throat.
This fear arrives
in the arms of violins
and Jew I remain,
standing in line
in a coat of moths,
in a coat of fog,
and the concert halts.

*

25

The early hour
tosses with
the semi-darkness
and tough shadows.
I reason
with my thumbs
and want to keep away
from obscure halls.
I can hear the cars
going perhaps everywhere,
golden in the early morning
and my friends sleep
the sleep of being close
to the museum.

*

Dead swans
drift in my imagination
and I take an early drink.
I take these legs
to dumbfounded churches
and weep for the fallen
gods of mourning.
And the sunlight
hovers like smoke
over a train
carrying some poet's
bones, smiling
into the future
ahead of me.

*

I accuse the world
of having stolen
the pigeons from
my window,
and beneath the benches
feed them cocktail sandwiches
from the night before.
I am Schwartz
the magnanimous,
smooth of wit,
facile, glib, and true
as a meteor
in my castigations.

*

I am the best
of my age,
its hands and eyes,
and say so
while the clock ticks,
forlorn
as the frosted grass.

Letter to a Professor of Spanish

Dear Jose,

My house is silent.
My father is doing some Spring planting,
My niece, nephew, brother-in-law and sister
are at church.
My mother walks the house like a stowaway
on her own ship.
Spring is so lovely.
And I am here flesh and bone,
half sad,
trying
to catch
the mystery
of thoughts
grabbing the air.
I am like a silent bartender
complaining about business
or a drunk violinist
walking
the morning
unsure yet dedicated
to a concerto of blue spiders
carrying his poems.

I attended my aunt's funeral
in Robstown, Texas.
I loved her so.
She was so gifted
with joy like a

sad waltz
or a cherubic
blanket.
The dead look so peaceful,
like the ocean.
Aunt Anita Rodrigues,
your death hurt.
We may see you again someday.
I doubt it.
The dead are on a train.
My fingers have the smell
of death.
My eyes.
My tongue.
Life ends like a clarinet;
it ends with a thud.
A footstep.
It ends like a beaten tongue.
Like a stolen shoe.
A horse without a rider.
A huge cracked bell
that doesn't tell
anyone where the mad live.

Letter to Leonard Adame

Now that the evening rain has gone
and a silence pervades like your arguments
against metaphysics, I conjure you
a theocrat in Tenochtitlan, smoothing the hair
of a princess or out searching the plaza
for the late delicacies of the night.
You call bird-like into the mist
and predict the migration of butterflies
with the silver notes of a flute;
the star of your eyes is dreaming ahead
to the calm prayer of the Spanish.
The moon sifts across your shoulders,
it is the coming of friendship into the house
of polemics and verse, and I purse my lips
like an Indian going out to the marketplace
for the first time in search of his brother.

Letter Left for Jon Veinberg

You must be out somewhere counting the trees or
the dreamers, the fireflies disappearing in October
with its treasures in a coat of dusk. I am welcomed
into your house by Moses, your dog, and the crickets
are serenading while the evening gathers its flesh
of children. I have wondered about Estonia, the blood
of your forefathers like a sky bluer than silence.
Under the stars I catch your warrior's laughter and
in the house of Estonia a last star traverses your eyes
in the hush of coffee and morning. You're a magician
in the clouds, sojourning through my life, a troubador
singing the simple odes to light. I wish I could
spin your heart through my Mexican barrio and joke
the mariachi into song, quibble about girls and
the nature of angels. You are a song. And the ballads
of the mountain and cornfield sing a joy of good fortune.
I too welcome dawn like you and whistle down the avenue,
confident, positive, the mid-noon sun will be a poem
written in the heart where it all belongs.

Soto Thinking of the Ocean

With the sun's
performance
dying slowly,
Soto thinks of
the ocean.

The powerful,
the weak
and the restless
inhabit
the shore
like drunk priests;
a puff of smoke
and a woman
full breasted
walks
the afternoon.

A crazy childhood
goes before us,
and Soto
is in the water again--
ointment
for youth,
old age
and belligerence,
blessings which
come our way
like goats
flushed from
the hills.

The ocean,
goddess,
immutable
temptress of water--
The incoming waves
catch us
in our
amazement,
that we are mortal,
that we could drown
near shore
and be remembered,
be recognized
like strong
tobacco,
and like pelicans
considered
in a strange way
romantics.

We are all being
beaten by the waves
under this
August sky.

Unsent Letter to Chris Buckley

The days drop like knives in the darkness
and I conjure you in a scholar's coat, drinking
beer and watching the dust-light spread.
I see the sweat on your forehead beading
nightdream in September and can think
of the lovely schoolgirls with their low-cut
blouses, nipples of ebony eyeing the world.
Friend to this crazy turbulence
in the heart, the night is opening like a cloud
and the autumn leaves fall in the staccato beat
of your voice, cadenzas in your soldier's heart.
May all your nights rub light against you
their oil of moonlight as you make your way
through the bashful barrooms and country walks,
sweetly singing the cosmos.

You Are Not Here
for B.H.

And I piece together this friendship
like dusk finding its way through
the blue eucalyptus and touching my hand.
I see your face like Rembrandt perhaps
saw his mistress, and then walked outside
to stroll the streets. I can be honest
as this distance of ours shortens into love
and the blossoms twirl their tongues.
There is music to your voice and
a child's silence in your amber breasts.
I wait like a Parisian in a coffee shop
not wanting to waste words, words that
are like sparrows and fly deathless
into you, their mouths caught in the twigs
of their philosophy. I have to tell you
there is no one on the veranda
picking flowers or filling the birdbath.
And to what pains we've bitten into.
They're a bell of clouds in the memory,
dreams which snared us beneath the trees.
And the evening walks off, shrugging
its grey shoulders, and I'm on a bench
impetuous as the pigeons pecking
the nothings in my hands, holding
a simple hat for your soul.

Poem before a Tremendous Drunk

I venture forth onto the avenue
like an avocado picker in search
of a woman. I am in an indelicate
cerebral mood, and the toxic
whispers of the starlings
keep my feet in bombastic
condition. I wish for once
to come upon this incredible
world and catch it by the nose,
toss it to the ground
and bedevil the evening
with young sarcasm.
Were I a Novelist,
I would wire the nearest
telegraph office I was
working on my third masterpiece
to send more money.
But poetry is like a drunk
starling and must be met
head-on like the avocado
picker I was supposed to be,
the one searching for a Madonna
to help him keep up
with the extravagant
insignificance
of us all.

III

Darkness under the Trees

With a candle half lit from the kitchen,
a dark woman on the phone, a mad woman
thinking about romance, a Japanese girl
who comes up to my shoulders, and a
polite hunchback for company...
Desperation flashes his white teeth.
A pistol in the closet.
Any of us could go under the darkness
of trees. A black dog and a white
cat keep vigil. Our prayers go
unheard in this twilight where
the roses droop around the thickness
of flies and the stench of another day.
How I weep for the fallen
and their gentle steps
catching me like a camera
which cannot focus on pain.
The neighbors drunk on silence
and gritos! for Cinco de Mayo.
I wish I could explain to God,
ask forgiveness, but I'm awkward
with the sentimental.
Don Quixote and I have lost
our minds--this is
another involuntary jump
into the darkness under the trees...

Falling

It has taken three
summers to sort out
my life.
Once fallen,
angels are known
to come back
with a graceful poise,
like that of a gazelle
or even an ant.

I fell for love
And what a thud--
Loud, tearful, insane.
She was beautiful.
I was an ass.
I have had incredible moments
of happiness,
anguish and sadness.
Between those times
I've been out in the meadow
on horseback
Bruised by deception
and the dream of water.
What more can I say
about the Lady
except she liked prunes.
An albatross fate
intervened,
wounding both of us
I thought it to be a tragic end
but I recovered thank God
for I fell like an angel.
I flew love's flight
and what's an angel without
wings.

Shoes

On this windy night
at a farm for losers
I imagine winners all night
drinking the night.
What a dismal day.
I want so much to look
the other way
but God won't let
me put on my shoes.

And My Presence Shut Away

A world away from you,
I'm angry at wetbacks
and the boredom which
pokes its finger
in my eye.
I could say I've become
accustomed
to the pestilence
of mediocre men,
to the sultry fire
of my ambitions.
But I'm miles away from
myself, and can hear the
dried up poetry
of the defeated.
On days like these,
when my heart
goes on horseback
above the doves,
I want to hold on
to a woman
and not let go.
I want my imagination
to attract something beautiful
and go to heights...
My thinking must be pure
for even the complacent
clouds of autumn
look forlorn,
and the ancient bards
have nothing to say anymore.

This keeps madness near my fingers.
I must do something soon
or this grotesque
and punishing afternoon
will close
with the darkness
starting under the trees...

Lover in a Mad World

I'm the crazy lover
in a mad world,
surviving on the mire
of kisses and sacrifices.

I have a rendezvous
with opinions, the rain
and my unmarried love.

I have the fingers of sickness
and the heart of an oak.
The fire of my mother's brain
given to celestial wires.

I'm a witness to the deaths
of elegant women,
those dreamt up
and those self caused.

In New York I look
down the Avenue of The Americas
and there are no more dreams--
no stutter of butterflies,
not one unholy bosom.

I'm the rebel, angel, ghost
of a blue within--
haunted, evil, angry and
perplexed by the young,
trying to smile over the abyss
asking a Christian God
to save me.

This May Morning

Someone is mowing his lawn
in the distance.
I am looking at a bunch
of cows wag their tails.
My schizophrenic friend
is thumbing through the mail,
a sudden, half-hidden terror
in his eyes.
The trees are
restless, I'm restless, and
the whole world is like
an old kettle drum,
moving slowly and capriciously.
The roosters are crowing.
The wind comes like a messenger
from the east, wishing us
all happy birthdays...

We're like a hopeless
bunch or rats
caught in their traps.
And Jesus in abeyance,
we're all thieves here.
The train is elegant,
easing our pains.
I wish we were on it.
All the mad need
is a ride somewhere.
And Beauty, she's off
somewhere taking a bath.
And I'm secretly hoping
for two days of rain.

A Fresh Start

I begin to tell it...
this morning breaks into my life
like a bleak pale stranger
who wants nothing, and begs
for life as if it added up
to something. And the silence
grows immaculate in my fingers
wanting to touch someone tender.
I wonder if love
is like an aperitif
turning one into a drunk
or some tubercular ghost
suddenly appearing.
I grieve the melancholy
of swallows and how the persimmon
tree outside is like an only child,
and I'm aware I'm alone.
And I'm walking sideways
in my many childhoods,
anarchist and lonely hunter
of the dark.
I could be saved from it all
but the clouds have nothing to say.
And my loves are so distant
that I must have made this story up.

I Want to Tell You

I want to tell you
what you are for me,
girl with the feet
of my many childhoods.

Your mouth
is a blossom of vermillion,
pigeons fluttering
morning into light.

It would be wonderful
to catch you.

I want to disappear into a rose
and come back to you.
As the afternoon lifts, I
say what a hell of a life.
Your body of blue wind
makes me crazy. I want
to dissolve into the slow burn
of your eyes. Eyes that lead
to desire, pull and tug at my legs
like children at a cemetery.
Your waist of water,
I want to drown there.

But this morning's rain is quiet
and mournful like the breath
of a bird, and somehow I've
got to shake this sadness

away. I've got death caught
in my throat, like the bones
of a needlefish, backslapping
me into illusions.
I see my forty year old face
in the mirror, there's static
on the air but a laconic hush
in the eyes.
My mother would be proud
to know my thirst for life
is finding its words.

This Is What I Said

"I'm a very metaphysical cat,
someday I'll be slicing apples
in heaven." I tell my companion
the Estonian. The night
is just right for this, and
he laughs, and we both laugh.
Deep inside me, I think
difficult thoughts and wonder
whether my intellect is sharp
enough for this, or if I can
translate the feeling that
overcame me when my grandfather died,
or the time I had a high fever
and saw ghosts in the garden
and my mother consoled me.

There was a time when I chased
butterflies in Mexico, and the
mad nearby grinned with huge
faces which seemed to be made
of my mother's apron.
I realize I'm nothing;
yet if something kind were
to come from nowhere,
I'd start believing all over
again, and smile at a girl's
fancifulness, gather myself,
and make a life.

The Odds

When the odds are against you
all you have to do is grin...
How does a man of substance
learn to divide and subtract?
But by paying attention
and simply trying. How does
anyone do anything? Even animals
have customs; I only wish
they could ask a perfect
question like what time is it?
or, when do I have to go to bed?
Going to bed is difficult, especially
if you don't have someone dear...

Let the dead-mad divide and
anger the moon, but I prefer
to simply go unadorned
among kings and hold my head
high among the common towns
I come from, unnoticed in my
open coat and summer hat.
I've known dogs in my life
who have died gallantly
with feet straight up in the air.

What Is This Something?

Mother, tomorrow I'm leaving for
San Francisco and I'm sadder
than the seagulls circling
your forehead. These hands
of sesame, go tranquilly
searching the kitchen table,
and I'm the loneliest of ghosts
sitting there waiting for
a breakfast of lumps and
hurts; pains on a voyage
to my shoulders, counting
twos and threes.

I'm in love but the madness
eating at me isn't love,
but something bigger like
a dark knife popping up
on the seashore, cutting
this heart.
I want desperately to bury
these eyes in the bluest
snow, catch the throat
of my shadow and fleece
its wool, make a coat
and go through the streets
silent, unnoticed, carrying
a big stick to beat the hat
of my soul carries since I've
forgotten to be a child.
I'm in love and the evening
tells, me NO, NO!
The woman too is afraid,
and I'm afraid, and the whole
world is grinning, bigtoothed
and crazy/cruel.

The Woman Who follows Me Home from the Park

I go to the park I love
where women in black
relax like forgotten madonnas,
and I talk to myself
in Spanish.

The sun leaves a piece
of gloom at twilight;
immersed in blue thought,
smoke trails me

to a bar where a woman
is putting on lipstick,
trying to avoid the tragedy
of the juke box and mirrors.
We sing to swallows
on their way to the graveyard
over silver martinis,

and soon I am fondling
a breast
on a mountain of bone;
the woman is ashen-faced,
the flower of evening
smelling of snow.

In the yellow dust
beyond the door,
girls dance
and carry smiles to town,
I groan under the bills of
mockingbirds,
twirl my tongue and whistle.

A wild guitar plays
over a green hill.
I separate my fingers
and lust flys
on black horses' hooves
by the road.

Evening

With a storm on the way
we sit outside
with the evening wind
at our side, imagining
vast utopias, bigger
than ourselves...
The evening gives us
no answer, neither
does the wind.
We just bleed inside
and look puzzled
through the trees.

There is a great sky above
and a future as bright as that sky,
lonely and honest.
I'm looking at the ants
in my laziness,
at their magnificent wisdom.
Not a thing wrong with me at the moment,
but a lackluster heaven, and a love
deeper than a ghost's tunic,
which could be purple and blue,
sashed in red silks.

I'm walking home after a restless day--
what settles in my mind
is the cool wind, a restive heart;
I hope to have been born for good;
in my ignorant way
I am studying history,
a blank page today
told me many things--
how to fold it and go on reading.

After I'm Gone

The room will smell of olives
and oleanders.
I will want to wake up
and see the rain,
touch some faces with my fingertips,
and apologize.
I will want music.
I will want to kiss the earth
and take my eyes to a Mexican
cemetery.

But the air will be blue,
my loved one will be dressed
in black, soused, and in tears.
On the far side of town
will be a band headed for the madhouse.
My sons and daughters will
be playing games.

The pages of my manuscripts
will blow loose
and turn into flies.
Everyone will be killing flies
and I'll be a romantic
again dreaming about crazy women
dressed in red.
I'll be quietly dreaming
again after I'm gone.

WALKING BEHIND THE SPANISH

I

To the Tavern Where Life Meets the Eye
I Turn an Ear and Boast Friendship

I am a friend to the fingers
of darkness and to the Spanish
ghosts I walk behind.
They haunt the tavern
where the lost drink
 and talk looking for saints.
I have sat with melancholy
 gazed into its eyes
 and felt its raw fingers
 on my neck.
 I am a friend of those
 that have been driven
to the stars for company
 and drink to them that
they may find their souls.
I have sat with beauty
and had it scuffle me to the ground
and pronounce me dead.
But I'm a friend
of the night
 and calmly greet its fellowship.
And live in the belly
 of the sky
 looking forward to my friends
who haunt the tavern
 with the granite weight
 of their dreams.

It Is Getting Cold in October

There is a road which leads me out of this poem.
A blushing woman bathes, she is looking for me.
The rose has become frightened, the petals
are looking inside of me.
A Mexican worker is smiling counting his money
the dirt on his face is America.
I am looking for my wife in a factory,
her eyes are hushed like my drugged feet.
The prostitute is eyeing her nipples,
they are defenseless, the men come to her
like fishermen who never go fishing.
A young man I know has slashed his throat.
The night grows in America.
A spider makes its web over my head.
I light a cigarette,
a dog barks.
It is getting cold.

What the Ocean Is Saying

You tell me that fate
is circling this house
like a mad wolf.
That my heart is green
and going skyward.
That my fingers
are walking
into the back of my head.
We are in love with death
you and I
like sleepwalkers
on a honeymoon.
Forlorn and weary
these eyes of yarn
go like fools
to watch you die.
And each day
the ocean comes closer
like a knife
or a gentle hunchback
in great loneliness,
touching your hand
in spite of everything.

The Road of El Sueño by the Sea

Thinking of the silent deaths by the sea
and of the beautiful women in Santa Barbara,
I stroll backwards into the heavens
of my soldier's face, poor aristocrat
in a town with too much money.
I secretly run my hand up a Greek
woman's bosom and drink to those
secrets that will never be mine.
I spun in crazy here looking for
the kharma I lost elsewhere.
A gentle ghost haunts the Taverna.
Have I discovered myself here?
Death looms in the distance
with bent ears, I'm going around
circles begging the night
to return to Santa Barbara
where the future
sways its fingertips,
and where we will be on the road
off el Sueño humming this
evening, the dream will be gone,
and the sea, the quiet bystander
to all this, will begin
to tune itself to a quiet madness.

My Dead Friends Are Hitchhiking

This day in September with the black
angels of death hovering above like dark mistresses,
my dead friends are hitchhikingg and ghosts
in the countryside dance.
I'm a passenger on a bus on the way
to the madhouse to see someone.
It's all familiar my coming here
the voice that said "All will be well,"
and the dark stranger who swore
Jesus would be back.
My friend is in another world preparing
for the next war. Should I tell him he
is already in one, that someone is going
to cover him with a sheet and not give
a damn. That his goings and comings
are for naught. Friend, on this day
I could write you a poem and you
couldn't understand. "No one understands,"
I mumble. I catch his eye; he knows.
The doomed shall be saved.

I Surrender in the March of My Bones

I surrender in the march of my bones
to another night, and am stung
 by the air which hums
delicately my name.
These words coming as confused
 larks to play games.
These hands
which are like spiders to my being
used to the lonely
 alienation of their web.
I am here night and day
in the fragrance
 of the crazy air,
in the shadow of the ghettos
 in the awkward palm
of poverty.
 Alone, I see
coffins with sails
 and winter's ghost
 walks on the pier.
The lovely women who must die
like broken dolls
and the hummingbird
with its
feminine heart
on the edge of insanity.
I surrender to the march of my bones
to another day,
 which feels for my throat
like the lost feet

of a nightingale.
 Inwardly I listen to the trembling
of the utter silence
and that life is passing
like a magician scattering stars.

Women Like Taverns I've Dreamt

I am a cow
and I am chasing you.
Soon I will turn
into a swan
and kiss
you.
If I pretend
long enough
I will eat you
raw,
then look for
you
somewhere in
my shoe.
If you're good
I'll look
inside
your eyes,
pass out
on your breasts
and ride a train
to the cemetery
where they will
bury all of us
like damned souvenirs
someone forgot
to open.
In the meantime
a haunted
woman

lures me
to her house
where a drunk
pigeon
hums lullabyes
and her lust
points at me
like the fingernail
of death.

The Garden

Someone has been weeping here,
attentive wrestling with the white bones
of humans.
Someone I know well with the swat
of these fingers I pronounce him dead.
What can I add
to this riddle?
It is shaking
my shoulder, it isn't me here
with these words damning my blood,
running with pointed head
through these closets.
No, it is the shaved head
of an owl, observing me
quietly through the long
impetuous night.
It is a woman come out to dance
adding insult to my fatherless brow.
It is something sleeping behind me.
It is everywhere
and I must go feeling its quiver
of nails on my feet.
Someone has been weeping here
among the flesh of bones,
bouquets, and a sinister laughter
flying around
like a gray galaxy of flowers.

The Air Goes Pushing Me Along

The air goes pushing me along,
to the tunes of seagulls.
I have blue houses in my hands,
their windows are rosebuds
and on the edge of night
God is in tears...
I will thrust through the pale
light of evening an echo,
long like the kiss of
a lover and show these
child's hands to a cloud.
I have the radiance of flight,
I think of the women who
will love their children.
I touch the blood of their hair
like any man, and silently
weep dark crevices of air.
I am fortunate like a blue daybreak,
and jump into tenderness
like a schoolboy.
I will die deep
like a drunk sailor,
I will die when the air
is a bad child, and my
face will be born with new flowers.
And the yellow light
from my pains will carry
a handsome note written
on a half opened pomegranate.
The moon with a washed face
will appear and a guitarist
will strum
verses. I'll go, love, like
blue butterflies.

The Night Air Brings No Message

Away from the university
listening to the tolling of bells
I try to make sense of what is here,
a box of oranges,
 moths playing cruel games
 with the light bulb,
 an epileptic woman
who writes letters,
 the patio which is aging
and my face
 which seems
to have forgotten itself.

My mind has seen too much
of the world,
 I have a quiet passion for order
but 3's and 4's don't add up
 and the night fails to calm me.
Away from the professors,
the hardheaded coeds,
 I've prospered into the same paths
as before,
 life is a maze
and amazement flashes a weak smile
Success--a piece of star which drowns
in the night air.
 And man's fascination with fame
walks like a hobo through
the barrio.
The world has no use for madmen;

self deception
grabs for the throat.
Disillusionment is thick,
the night air brings
no message from home.
I've dreamed myself:
even the dogs are lonely.

Quietly

No more sadness
to greet me,
but the ocean
with its face
of guitars.
A clown on
the road
laughing
under the trees.
A young woman
with the feet
of doves
chooses
to be silent.
And the dead are so
quiet, to visit
them is like
visiting
a star.
And I want to
thank someone.
Kiss a woman softly
on the lips
and disappear
somewhere
dancing
quietly.

Purgatory

I am a witness
to the death
of shadows,
and lunge
at them
in chaos.
One has my
shoes in its mouth,
the other is holding
my hat.
I want to declare victory
over them,
but am left taking
drags
from a cigarette,
confused.
Life has a hold
of my legs.
I wander
trying to reason
evil away,
and come
up
with mud on my hands.
My spirit takes leaps,
I am going through
a terrible time.
And like a wounded animal
I take hold again.

When We Have To

An evening stroll
has declared me sane
for the world.
The hurried days
walk beside
me like stray dogs;
I've invented
no one today,
no ghost to walk beside
me and act as a shepherd
in the night.
Left this way
to the motion of flowers
and lovers who
have shunned me,
I discover
the air--
air is air
yet the arithmetic
of birds
with their songs
becomes
like my waltz,
unheroic...
With the cry of the mudlark,
all bitterness
leaves
as if starbound
knowing
we shine in the paleness
when we have to.

II

I Salute the Dead

In this drunken town
bitten by the whores
of Texas, I pause with
a beer to salute the dead.

Someone's in my house
--the dead child of Texas
haunts the woodwork
and the child is everywhere
tonight waiting for the dawn,
tomorrow maybe playing
in the mud.

My nephew asks if the black
children he sees on TV
are the poor, and I reply,
"We are the poor."
He cannot understand,
and I know this house
is as poor as this drunken
town
and I drink my beer and
hiccup into song.

Ode to Those Things I'll Leave Behind
I Suppose Love Has Always Troubled the Philosophers
for D.W.

What have I got to look forward
to God, but the full moon
looking over things
and the dogs wailing country
style?
What but to listen to my own
song, and take in the symmetry
of the countryside.
My aristocratic neighbor
he knows everything
and his wife squeals
under his roof, I have
no one and go about my business.

The night is immense
without love.
People forget us.
I can think of Maria
burdened and waiting
as if each man were
an answer.
Of the Dulcineas
that go drunk through
life, defeated
like an ache.
Of the swallows in the moon's light
and of my youth
which went intrepidly
like a sleepwalker.
But now I falter
quixotically,
and the stars
take human form
in my emptiness.
Middle age teaches us to

be careful,
and when a sensitive woman
comes along
not to hang on to the sky
or try to dress a cloud to her fancy.
I suspect I'm a perfectionist
in these matters,
which accounts for much
of my loneliness.

But women are the moon's
lost children,
and can make life
miserable.
To take them with
a scar of salt
is about all one
can do.

I'll never find
the one I want,
death woke me early
like a thief
but to make life
seem less mad
is a task,
and when life goes off
like a careening
bus,
take to the self
those things you need
and leave all else behind.

Falling and Remembering

Listening this gray Tuesday
to little philosophers, finches--
rebels who gather each morning
reminding me of the dead.
I am here like an introverted
rose, stoic, quiet in bloom,
knowing the petals will fall
like some drunk in a cantina.
Afternoon too is falling
like a tiny God with no name,
and I'm falling and the slow
wind is bending the shoots
of plants like my heart thinking
of dying. There is no escape--
a fly buzzes my ear reminding
me I must stop this.

If You Want to Know Something about Me Talk to the Clouds for I Am Going There

I'm going to paradise
I tell my friends,
to brag again
and love.
My disconsolate
female companion
wants to tag along,
to live utter
bohemians,
eking along
to the beat
of a train
to the brash
bravado
of poetry
smiling
like a woman's breasts;
and the kisses of angels
on the way
shall make
the road
bitter,
mad, lovely
like a turning
soft voice
of the madonna.
It shall find me
in cafes, brothels,
madhouses,
universities.

Open-collared
and friendly,
ready to eat
lightning,
sing to the bitches
with wings
who fly in and out
of my life.
For I will be driven
into the clouds,
with a fat finger,
a goddamned fatalist
is here
sitting on snow
with melancholy hands
ready to rip
out the sweet heart
of a nightengale.

A Bit Crazy

I'm growing fonder
of the light
which has pierced
this heart of olives.
Like a huge hand
that wears shoes,
like a lighthearted woman
out to the opera.
Darkness has scattered my clothes,
my poems.
Evening salutes
like an admiral,
my heart is among the trees
in laughter.
I leave my solitude
holding on
like a scared prostitute,
and amble on
a little stage frightened,
the world looking on,
the small applause of stars,
as my heart tips its hat...

The Town with No Dreams

I linger in the cafe
where the last angel has left
unimpressed with the world.
I live like a lark on the edge
of thunder where Aztec ghosts
conjure in my mind the lost
paradise. It is not enough
that I am here consul of rain,
mathematician of lost love
for here the heart is
blunted by boredom and disenchantment.
My rebel head leaves the street
as a dream giving its adieu
to other dreams
which once kept me afloat.
Now the terror comes at me
in bits dressed in sunlight
like a betrayer. I have a foot
inside a flower and the clouds
are busy writing death notices.
The town never wakes from its
illiterate sleep, I pause
and sidestep beggars
looking for someone to poke
me in the ribs and wake me from
this dream.

The Mind Does Wander

Alone to the tinkering
of my mind,
I am swept away
aloof and interested
in the life
of birds, shadows
and the ghost
which follows me
with a lantern
through the street.
I am immersed
in self delusion
and the walls
of my room
creak
with insomnia.
Someone is chasing
me up my arm.
I put on my
best shirt
to see my doctor.
Life hides from me
like a punished dog.
Will I ever walk
out of this madness?

I Live Among the Shadows

With the backdrop
of lovers in the meadows,
this beaten heart
asking to be dropped
like fruit from
a tree,
I go again
into the shuffle
of my mind,
somewhat weatherbeaten,
carryinng a shadow
through the fields...

This is the fictional
rendition of my life--
I am the blind organ player,
none of the keys are white,
none black, the music
somehwere in between...

And when I think
of the afterlife,
a trail of breadcrumbs
leads back to itself,
fattening the grey birds
that ask nothing of me
but circle all day
in the near, blue distance...
sometimes I think I
could throw a stone,

a coin, the silver bracelet
with my name, sometimes,
my shirt is no defense,
and the birds are vague
as an itch on the lover's
backs in the field, or stars
behind the clouds of night,
sometimes they are as vague
as my eyes, as the one road
of the lost, as my empty hands...
I must have left something,
somewhere.

A Clever Magician Carrying My Heart

October comes with its awful
arms about to explain to me
life's troubles. In the garden
the woman is breathing roses
and the sky is on horseback
opening like a huge bone.
And throw these words
at trees, crickets and a wounded
dove. There is a stillness
about, and a crazy, shadow
tilling the soil.
My loves go like butterflies
through my eyes and I count
the kisses which have turned
to water. Everything is leaving
like an owl witch hunting
in the night.
My life walks in with
the torn pages of these
shadows in mime.
And a clever magician
struts through the street
carrying my heart.

Rosita, the Future Waits With Hands of Swans

To the vile drumbeat of evening
dressed in fine silks,
to an awkward offbeat
a wave of ocean water,
I escape among the little gods
of moonlight the castaway.
To the kiss of the imaginative
woman, the hard knock
of her eyes, the petulant
grief imbedded in us all--
I smile, the tolerant
hellish gesticulator
of the brainy night.
In whose hands we do
leave that softness,
killing us.
In what twist
do I leave Rosita
whose life batters
the insane flies of romanticism.
In whose blood do we sing?
And what if the moon sent
a messenger with round
impecuous eyes to take
our hands.
Rosita's bloody wrists
the trumpet blares in her eardrums.
Do I listen to this cumbia
or do I take my Aztec
hands to forecast

the future intelligence
of Cuauhtemocs.
I shall find you in Tocalitlan,
my Mexican wife,
in a very gorgeous gown.
Rosita, face to face,
what will you tell me?

Visitors from the Afterlife

I am visited by the mad angels
of light,
crazy spooks of laughter
with their smile,
and strange dumbstruck
quips.
Like a shouting bird of daybreak
I am their captive,
in this fancy clairvoyance
I am on an itinerary
of timetables
with the frenzy of the owl.
They have come to save
me from the world of mad machines.
Then comes the afternoon
with its dazzled melancholy.
It has the mouth of a child,
rapturous
misanthropic.
My imagination
keeps the mad angels festered
in my brain,
they are the harmless elves
of my childhood
grown up.
They are God-sent
and people my darkness;
they are the hermits
of the afterlife
and I welcome them.

My Quixotic Bang Up
(The tragedy which broke me open)

There is a full moon
tonight and I am
as confused as
the lark.
Could it be
because
the moon houses
the mad?
Or is it
loneliness
stretched out
on the porch
like a cat.
I am in this labor
of life tasting
a resin
which is unlike a woman.
I lite a cigarette--
the moon looks like
it is in terrible pain,
the insides of trees
are bleeding,
this house
is going to be eaten by darkness
the dogs are as sad
as the last oranges of winter,
and I'm coming back from it.
Back from the temptress
back from the mad.
I am a romantic
but I've had it up to my ears
listening to the damned.

I want no more madness
Lord.
That suffering
of imbecilic
homocidal moons,
 that rebellion of stars
 in the quiet nights
of searching.
I who want the depth
of harmony
 have found compassion
among the deaf
 and crazy;
now with the road
winding its fingers
 like a composer,
 I poeticize
the gentle spirit
 of this quixotic bang up.

After Your Absence

In a cloud with two angels
 comes the face of my mother;
and I've seldom spoken of you.
In your absence your son
has turned handsome.
This afternoon
with the sun about to leave
like you left me with your
sad poems in your lungs,
I pause and don't know
how to ever face you again.
I could have gone with
you ten years ago, but I
feel the music
you must have felt
when you were young
and beautiful.
The facts are I've been
terribly miserable inside,
and I've tried to hide it
 like one holding the hand
of strangers.
Your sisters are alive
and getting old.
Your daughter has two
children. Father
remarried, and is still
the same, with a gusto
and love for the restless.
Oh, I write poetry
now, mother.
You won't have to worry
I've got good friends
in addition to God.

We Shall All Meet Again
under the Cooing of Doves

Here it is the first of April
and I was supposed to be defeated
a long time ago.
I'm staying clear
of adultery
this time.
And with my nose clean
what comes after pain,
will coo
like doves
above
this madness.
I wish to leave
nothing behind,
just the road,
a glass of cognac
and these poems which
love everybody.

III

I'm Walking behind the Spanish

eavesdropping on their conversation:
Neruda sound asleep,
Juan Ramon placing yellow flowers
in his kitchen.
Miguel in jail.
Lorca playing flamenco
to a house full of romanceros.
Cesar Vallejo walking through
the streets of Paris.
I walk behind you
carrying this heart
of white rain which has
come out of the barrio
with the turbulence of
the Guadalquivir.
The sun is a witness
to your coming and going
like soldiers marching
towards the sea.
And this petty inquisitive
brain has watched you
enter my life.
Miguel weeping.
Lorca clean shaven and alert
murdered standing.
Neruda calm like dropping fruit.
Juan Ramon Jimenez
in a portrait of yellow flowers.
And Vallejo drunk with the ghost
of compassion, sipping cold coffee.

Behind time I'm
like a lost finger
in the sea.
Thrashing about
looking for a lost heaven.
I go dizzy through the crowds
whispering a tender
 folktale as if to a ghost.
I'm taking everything
to the sea, toss bird bones
there, eat bread and hold on.

*

I'm walking behind
the Spanish in a Madrigal
 dream,
The cow lays down,
the worker goes home
to his wife of complaints.
The banker can't spend
his money.

*

I lead a tragic life
but I have the optimism of
the owl.
Forlorn diplomat
of my existence

I go in soldier fashion
through life--
scarred, foolish
and romantic.
Making the best
of what is there.
And feel the tug
of angels in my footsteps.

Someone Is Buried
for Federico Garcia Lorca

The children are going to the clouds
to hear flamenco,
and there's a loud roar in heaven, Lorca.

They're still firing bullets, damnit,
and the world's on fire.

Women are passing, counting the dead--
horsemen with knives in the thicket.

Someone is being buried.
Black ribbons under an anonymous moon
and the wrong face under our blessings.

In heaven an angel fixes his trousers.
In Granada, the bells are tolling.

Someone is being buried.
There is no marker on your grave
in Granada, Federico Garcia Lorca.

Letter Too Late to Vallejo

This is the letter that couldn't get to you
because you were looking for food in Paris.
To your frail October bones I phrase my lines
like spokes in your heart of silver, and condemn
loneliness, fools, idle walkers through an immense rain.
There is a crimson hue to your cloud, bloodless
in the sky and giving like a child. There is a pallor
on your forehead the years won't take away
and a huge meteor circling the night of insomnia,
and you're taciturn, a quiet constellation of grit
and hope in the vapor of one more night alone.
Your Peruvian soul grieves like a cistern in a warehouse
of love, and the toxic moody eyes of one who's seen hell
and disappeared to heaven on the arithmetic of air.
You never returned to Peru, the University where
your fervid muscles ached like stars on their way
to jail. I see your hunger and metaphysical black angels
working around you and an impulse says, "Everything
will end soon on a Thursday in the rain."

Ode to Cervantes

You who died poor
tasting the very juices of fame
hero of war and philosophy,
the barroom and brothel,
the dungeon and Spanish stars.

This night of utter misfortune
and misery I want to pay homage
to your creation, your orphan,
your son--
that gentle knight of madness
using his helmet as a soup bowl
like any shining itinerant.

Miguel Saavedra Cervantes
brawler of the countryside.
My saint this connnubial
blundered night
of catastrophic mistakes
and a tilted will.

I want to take you to my heart
find a vein of poetry there
and follow it like the Guadalquivir
through the widowed plains.

I of sound mind
and wind in my logic
want to go against the State,
be imprisoned there,
and give compassion
to the luminous underdogs.

Let them speak of asylums,
of ghosts, of pain and rejection--
let God give us the constant struggle,
bread, and pursuit of dreams.

Cervantes, I want to touch
your bones and not bitch
about poverty anymore.

God is with me.
My friends are with me,
even if the people do not know
of this sadness,
which has built a path
inside my soul
on which I've traveled up and down
wrestling the white ghost of literature
and aristocratic circles.

I follow you
through little towns
with heartaches annd ballads
in their church steeples,
those roads of woe,
the holy gardens and cantinas
of lost design, ladies,
and the magnanimous folly
beneath a huge and wonderful sky.

Ode to Miguel Hernandez

Sitting quietly by the rivers
of summer, I pause and think,
"The Spanish are gathering their
speech in the clouds." The rustle
of trains backing into your soul
and those awful brooms standing
corpselike in the courtyard of
prisons, have no use for your
poems with their dove flight
to everywhere. No, not even your
bones on the neck of a bull would
begin to forget. I blame the
evening like a malignant stranger
straying into a battlefield, with
the blood of snow melting your
mouth into forgotten fields of
poppies. And those trains
of the wounded, bound and gauzed
in purple clouds exclaiming
the Republic. On a day like this
you are walking through the countryside
with Ramon Sije, writing your betrothed
and not realizing an end
to all your prismatic dreams.
I take your sheepherder's speech
and make a prayer in July,
and damn misfortune, brooms, silences,
and go with the pain into the storm,
and with this ode, forget myself...

Juan Ramon Jimenez in Heaven

You in your baroque home
in heaven--a cloud is a huge hand
in the sky, a lace cuff
over Catalina.
I with my butterflies
listen to their gossip.
Ramon, your poems were brought
to me by a swallow.
Death isn't so bad
 is it, Ramon? You who
have full use of your estate.
I with my madrigals move
to and fro, entertained
by a music from
God knows where.

For Good Pablo

We will in all certainty
try to be near to you.
For out of the clarion,
Chilean earth, cherubed
with wine, you intoxicated us,
you modeled a planet
for the desperate heart;
you, who talked to the stars
as if women lived there.
You who bathed your sea-
going hands with the blue
of agility and genius
in the emotion of earthen-
ware.
I can see you,
on a train with Miguel, Cesar,
Garcia, Rafael, Juan Ramon--
eating paella
on the edge of the horizon.
And describing the death
of Capitalism.
We will in all certainty
try to be there
when the day comes
trumpeting like a general
in the dust of Guernica.
the dust of tubercular
Miguel's bones,
the skull of Lorca
and the earth that will
become seed of us yet
about to fly and cover
the planet with blood.

When the Stars Get Angry and Coo above Our Heads
for the Generation of Spanish Civil War Poets

When the stars coo above
our heads like stragglers
in the sky and the birds
talk a strange language
I think of the absent.
Like a stranger
walking the streets
with the wounded
eyes of the swallow
I talk to absence.
They are gone
and the countryside
lies bare
before me
like a missing child
some metaphor
dumbstruck in a Spanish
ballad.
Death struck like a bone
in the wind knocking
senselessly about.
It took Cesar
in the crazy insomniac
night.
It bit Lorca in pieces
under the Falangist moon.
It walked in to Juan Ramon
like a woman wanting romance.
It crawled
from an immense crevice
in the earth
and chose Miguel.

It lunged at Neruda
like a barefoot
accordionist.
When the stars coo
above our heads,
the absent are about
and the strange sound
in the evening
 looks at the nude heart
of poetry in the bare
corners of all our rooms.

As I Look to the Literate

With small steps of amazement,
I go foolish into life,
foggy brained with the music
of oblique miracles.
The facts are plain, leatherminded
and scallawagged, but sensing
greater truths from them,
I am glimpsed at from
without--and a sure-footed
Cervantes lives in me
a wispy spider's flight.
Pleased with the nonsense
I've conjured, the night
air falls into my
lap of dreams.
As I fill this heart with
this dry language,
I focus
on the ordinary mathematics
of living, and go about my business
like a serious man
with a pencil behind
my ears.

A Night with Cervantes

We were talking mostly
about what we could do
not to disturb dreams.
 We sat long hours with drafts
of our work, discussing
a way to free the mad.
He was tall and lean,
 and very friendly.
He showed me his horse
and his battle scars.
I showed him a melancholy
ode on humility.
 A few goats walked in
to the taverna,
 and we drank and
ate unmindful of them.
I asked Sancho
what he thought
of literature and
he said, "It is
 a rose burning
 in the evening."
So we grabbed the bottle,
followed the goats outside,
and waited for the day
to burn away,
the rest of our lives
to find us
like the intemperate stars
imagining themselves into constellations.

The Ghost of Emiliano Zapata

This Sunday at the Market
with the clouds
like guerillas,
and the people
dove-like
approaching
as if from
the mountains,
the ghost of Emiliano
Zapata haunts
the market place.
This Sunday
the churches
are markers
 for graves,
and the insane
silence
rides a horse
to some heaven.
The woman across from
me wants to
be a mother
and I am full
of ambition.
The multiplication
        table of the poor
begins here
and the multiplication
of the dead ends
here as well.

Life on all fours
gets up
and lifts
itself like
a tired woman.
A hush enters
my lungs peopled
with darkness.

When This Life No Longer Smells of Roses

It will be raining,
the air will be blue,
my compadres will be
singing rancheras
and seagulls will be
dancing the "Jarabe."
My loved one will come
all the way from Paris;
my creditors will
denounce me.
Children will be
thrashing pinatas
and in the barrio
they will be singing
"Por Una Mujer Casada."
A would-be nun
will slash her wrists.
A gypsy will have
his guitar stolen.
My poems will turn up
in Mazatlan, starched
as napkins in good cafes,
and I'll be rehearsing
a ballad by Negrete,
dreaming of villages,
the white breasts
of the sea, and there will
be plenty of laughter.
When this life no longer
smells of roses,
I'll have left
on a tour with Don Quixote--
I'll leave no forwarding
address.

115

My Father Is a Simple Man

I walk to town with my father
to buy a newspaper. He walks slower
than I do so I must slow up.
The street is filled with children.
We argue about the price
of pomegranates, I convince
him it is the fruit of scholars.
He has taken me on this journey
and it's been lifelong.
He's sure I'll be healthy
so long as I eat more oranges,
and tells me the orange
has seeds and so is perpetual;
and we too will come back
like the orange trees.
I ask him what he thinks
about death and he says
he will gladly face it when
it comes but won't jump
out in front of a car.
I'd gladly give my life
for this man with a sixth
grade education, whose kindness
and patience are true...
The truth of it is, he's the scholar,
and when the bitter-hard reality
comes at me like a punishing
evil stranger, I can always
remember that here was a man
who was a worker and provider,

who learned the simple facts
in life and lived by them,
who held no pretense.
And when he leaves without
benefit of fanfare or applause
I shall have learned what little
there is about greatness.

I Am America

It's a hell of a world.
I go like a schoolboy stepping
through the murderous countryside,
a bit of rhyme, a little drunk
with the wonderful juices of breasts,
and the magnificent
with their magician-like words
slipping into the voice of America.
I carry my father's coat,
some coins,
my childhood eyes in wonder--
the olive trucks plucky
in their brash ride
through the avenue,
the wino in a halo of freedom,
the shopkeepers of Democracy.

I am brave, I am sad
and I am happy with
the workers in the field,
the pregnant women
in ten dollar dresses,
the night air supping
and stopping to chat
like a wild romantic lady.
Children's voices and dogs,
the bar, the songs and fights.
I go ruminating in the brothels,
the ghettos, the jails.
Braggart, walking into early
cafes confessing naivete
and love for the unemployed.

I'm a dream in the land
like the Black, Mexican, Indian,
Anglo and Oriental faces
with their pictures of justice.
I go gaudy into movie house,
flamboyant spectator
of horse races.
I am not unloved, or unwanted
but I have seen the faces
of the rebel, the outcast,
I have touched the madness, all the terrible
and I have seen the ghosts of the past.
I am a friend to all,
for I have touched everything,
even the empty plates of the poor.

I put on my clothes, my hat,
I visit everywhere--
I go to market for bananas,
smoke the air,
breathe America.

I am wretched and mean,
I am kind and compassionate.
I remember catechism class,
the nuns and the priests,
my sister's wit,
and the neighbor's beautiful wife.
I am walking behind America,
suspicious, pie-eyed,
open-faced in the distance.

I am a father of prayers,
obedient,
I am a father of women,
a son of women.
I speak as the common man
and listen like the wise.
I am America,
and by hearts grown cold to me
I will be the seer of my intellect.
I will put an end to misery with
the bravado of the seeker,
drunken, reveling
in this American continent,
tight fisted,
exposed like a blue rose
to the night stars.